take 10 to grow

take
10
to
grow

Franklin D. Cordell, Ph.D.
and
Gale R. Giebler, Ph.D.

Argus Communications • Allen, Texas

Cover Design by Gene Tarpey

Illustrations by George Hamblin

FIRST EDITION

© 1978 Argus Communications

Printed in the United States of America.

ARGUS COMMUNICATIONS
A Division of DLM, Inc.
One DLM Park
Allen, Texas 75002

International Standard Book Number 0-89505-017-X
Library of Congress Number 78-60169

0 9 8 7 6 5 4 3 2

Thank you Louise, Frank, Karen, Bill, and John. We express our heartfelt appreciation to you. You constantly inspire and support our personal growth. You supported our efforts with kindness, patience, and encouragement throughout the development of this book. We genuinely love you.

CONTENTS

1 **THE PROMISE OF PERSONAL GROWTH • 9**

- Living Adventurously
- The Effects of Living Life as an Adventure
- Life Goals as the Focus of the Adventure
- Learning to Control Your Time
- Building a Competent Self-Image

2 **PLANNING FOR PERSONAL GROWTH • 18**

- Exploring the Good Life
- Listing Life Goals
- Appraising Your Goals
- Planning Activities
- Building the Support You Need

3 **TAKING COMMAND OF YOUR LIFE • 35**

- Controlling Your Own Time
- Structuring Your Time
- Discovering Your Week

4 **BUILDING CONFIDENCE BY RECOGNIZING SUCCESS • 55**

- Exploring Your Self-Concept
- Maintaining and Changing Your Self-Concept
- Building a Success Journal

5 **SELF-ASSESSMENT, GROWTH, PROJECTS, AND BELIEFS • 73**

- Looking at Yourself
- Planning a Growth Project
- Creating a New World
- Growth-Producing Beliefs

7

6 SELF-ACCEPTANCE • 84

- Exploring Your Beliefs
- Success Fantasy
- Disputing Unwanted Beliefs
- Building a Growth Project
- Success Journal

7 FRIENDSHIPS • 100

- Looking at Your Relationships
- Self-Correcting Relationships
- Success Journal

8 YOUR RESERVOIR OF STRENGTH • 116

- Building Emotional Strength
- Success Journal

9 TOMORROW IS NOT GOOD ENOUGH • 130

- Determining Unfinished Business
- Clearing the Air
- Finishing Unfinished Business
- Acquiring Necessary Skills
- Success Journal

10 TIME TRAVEL • 149

- Dealing with the Past and the Future
- The Desire for Punishment
- Building a Positive Future
- Living in the Present
- Success Journal

11 CHERISHING YOUR ENVIRONMENT • 168

- Being Connected to Your Environment
- Success Journal

12 COMMITMENT TO LIFE-LONG GROWTH • 179

- Learning Is Magic
- Creating and Growing
- Success Journal

the promise of personal growth

In his explorations of human health, Pulitzer Prize winner Rene Dubos speaks for a growing number of scientists when he defines health as not just biological fitness but also a measure of each person's ability to do what he or she wants to do and become what he or she wants to become. More and more people are seeing success, happiness, and fulfillment—critical elements of health—as the natural heritage of every human person rather than as the province of a few. This new concept of human health is exciting because it brings the promise of personal freedom, joy, and fulfillment to everyone.

The process of becoming healthier is now more clearly understood as an adventure that starts with an

9

exploration of self and moves out through a series of larger and larger circles. The innermost of these circles contains only self, followed by those that include family, friends, and eventually the whole human race. This exploration of self allows us to discover how we are part of humanity's natural heritage, how we realize our potential by our own intelligent choices, and how our behaviors and feelings are related to those of other people.

LIVING ADVENTUROUSLY

"Adventure" is a word that means something different to almost everyone. To some people it means excitement—the joy and personal freedom that come with going to new places and doing new things. For these people, adventure brings a sense of power and competence, a sense of being connected to and in love with their environment. It means overcoming the fear of intimacy and relating to friends in close and tender ways. But most of all, adventure is a highly stimulating and exciting way of life.

Other people look at adventure from a negative point of view. They can see danger in adventure and, feeling fear, avoid it. There certainly are dangers in our

adventures, but many people blow them out of all proportion and freeze themselves in fear.

All of us make minute-by-minute choices. Either we choose to live in an adventurous way, or we seek security. When we choose security, we trade off excitement, joy, freedom, and power for a guarantee that our life will be predictable and manageable. But security comes at a high price—the price of a routine and sometimes powerless life, for which we can blame no one but ourselves.

THE EFFECTS OF LIVING LIFE AS AN ADVENTURE

The human potential astounds the scientist and the philosopher alike because it so far exceeds the average person's performance. If we look at just our biological capacities for a moment, we are amazed by our fantastic potential. Think of the brilliant, creative dancers and athletes you have watched. They are constant proof of humanity's potential for spontaneity, flexibility, and modification. The human body is a marvelous machine that can be taught to respond to training and conditioning immediately and automatically.

But physical development does not end with physical conditioning. We know that certain Hindu yogis and others can, through their powers of concentration, control their blood pressure, heartbeat, and skin temperature. Some are able to walk across beds of hot coals without burning their feet.

What are the outer limits of physical potential for the human being? What are they for you? How can you approach that potential? These questions lead to others: What are the outer limits of social and moral development? How can you approach them? We all know of people who have learned to love themselves and others in an unselfish way, who feel so close to the human race that they no longer fear loss of love, who are no longer intimidated by the comments that others make, and who can give freely of themselves and bring a powerful moral force to any human relationship. Fully moral people tell the truth, ask outright for what they need, and express themselves in free and spontaneous ways because they no longer fear rejection. Their identification with the human race gives them the ability to transcend time and to see that all people are much the same.

Highly moral and social people—those who are mature in the highest meaning of the word—are spontaneous and comfortable in their environment. They have highly aware, loving relationships with other human beings. They are tuned in to subtle changes and have a warm appreciation for the beauty of their environment.

The manner in which people relate to themselves can be developed far beyond what might normally seem possible. Many people feel that their emotional lives are out of control, that feelings of loneliness, anxiety, and boredom must crash over them like waves on the beach. But those who have developed a relation to themselves can sort through those feelings, keeping the ones that are positive and dismissing those that are negative. Mature individuals can deal with fears and guilts and can focus upon problems without distorting perceptions or allowing wishful thinking to color behavior. They have control of themselves and their own destinies. They respect themselves and live with themselves in a positive, loving relationship. They truly live life as an adventure.

Adventurous people learn to deal with work in a positive way and use it as a tool in their own self-fulfillment, seeking stimulation and growth through good work. They learn the joys of problem-solving and the excitement that comes with accomplishing a task. They take a broad view of their work; they can put up with the sometimes boring initial phases of a job because they see themselves progressing toward more interesting, more creative, more socially useful work.

Adventurous individuals are highly creative, filled with energy to be used in the here and now. They are highly spontaneous, not in an uncaring fashion but in a

13

positive way. They have flexibility of mind and the courage to affirm something new of value—to be out in front of the masses of people, alone and savoring that aloneness. They are willing to make mistakes because they have positive relationships with other people and because they know that mistakes are a natural part of the journey of life and need not provoke feelings of guilt or fear of punishment.

Those who are adventurous have an openness to everyday experiences that comes from their loving relationships with the environment. They are expressive, giving free rein to the broad range of their feelings and experiences. They do not fear self-disclosure but rather delight in expressing themselves to other people. They evidence a natural kind of wisdom in their relationships with other people and with themselves—a kind of power linked with humility, a goodness that comes from comfort and security in their environment, with little fear of breaking rules.

LIFE GOALS AS THE FOCUS OF THE ADVENTURE

Many people today are confused about what they want to do with their lives. They are often so indecisive that they burden themselves with anxiety and emptiness. They feel they want to go everywhere at once or want to be somewhere else but are not sure just where. Well-planned life goals can provide a sense of balance and direction. Although life goals often start with a fragile dream, they can flourish into brilliant reality by intelligent action.

Many healthy things happen when you learn to clarify and organize your life goals in order of importance, then choose daily activities to achieve those goals. You gain an important sense of power in your life. Your anxiety and emotional emptiness vanish, because knowing where you are going gives you a sense of progress which allows you to wrap up unfinished business and develop a feeling of confidence and achievement. Planning your life course is a crucial first step in the process of personal growth.

LEARNING TO CONTROL YOUR TIME

Two important questions need answering before you attempt to set up a program for personal growth: How can you find time to get involved in a program? How do you break the routine you are already locked into?

For most of us the time between getting up in the morning and going to bed at night is filled with continual activity, some of which is happy and productive but some of which is simply a waste. The only time available for personal growth is the time you make by specifically including it in your schedule or by using the time you have more efficiently. This means cutting out

some routine (possibly self-defeating) and mindless activities and including more activities that move you toward your goals. This can be done by looking at your responsibilities and at what you want to do and, based upon that examination, consciously structuring your time.

BUILDING A COMPETENT SELF-IMAGE

As you plan your life goals and make choices about how to use your time, you call up in your mind an image of yourself and choose to do things that are consistent with that image. Sometimes this promotes growth, but sometimes not. If you see yourself as an adventurous, skillful, competent, and lovable person, you will act with courage and love. If you see yourself as a limited, unskilled, and unlovable person, you will act in a frightened and destructive way in conformity with that image. In that case, personal growth means changing your self-concept.

Your self-concept was formed and is maintained by means of a complex process starting with the names people gave you and what they told you about yourself. When you were very young, your parents probably told you in a dozen different ways that you were good or bad, successful or unsuccessful. You believed them, and that is how your self-concept got started. It has since grown and been maintained by the things you tell yourself and notice about yourself. If you tell yourself you are limited, you reinforce your feelings of fear and limitedness; if you pay attention only to your failures, you maintain an image of yourself as a failure. In your routine, unconscious activity you tend to reinforce your self-concept, whatever it is; but in your conscious self, you can recreate that image into a more productive one.

In order to intentionally create a positive self-concept, you must learn three skills:

1. You must recognize that what others told you about yourself was not always accurate.
2. You must learn to make your self-talk (the things you tell yourself about yourself) positive and constructive.
3. You must learn to notice the fine, beautiful, and loving things you do rather than your mistakes and inadequacies.

RECOMMENDED READING

Moustakas, C. *Loneliness and Love.* Englewood Cliffs, N.J.: Prentice-Hall, 1972. Here Moustakas explores the experience of loneliness. He discusses the battle "to be" and explores the ideas of being alone and lonely, showing that the individual is always in a struggle to develop self as a separate entity but is at the same time seeking to belong to the group.

————. *Personal Growth.* Cambridge, Mass.: Howard Doyal, 1969. In this short book the author looks at the process of personal growth from an existential point of view. He explores some of the causes of alienation in our society and shows how personal responsibility is the basis for personal growth.

17

planning for personal growth

The adventure of personal growth is born with a dream but is realized through intelligent planning and thoughtful action. The exacting business of translating dreams into specific goals and goals into specific actions is essential to personal growth.

There are four basic steps you must take as you attempt to translate dreams into goals and goals into plans:

1. You must clarify your life goals by exploring your personal image of the good life, then listing all the things you want out of life.

2. You must organize your life goals in order of importance. This forces you to make some hard choices—to eliminate some goals and put others on the back burner.

3. You must draw up workable plans that will help you achieve your important goals by thinking of *specific* things you can do to achieve them. (This often means building a support system, learning to manage your time more efficiently, and learning to communicate more effectively with others. More about this in later chapters.)

4. You must organize your plans into activities you can start now, as well as activities you will need to engage in later.

That sounds like a real challenge, and it is. But the rewards are in proportion to the effort. Effective planning helps you build a commitment to growth that ultimately makes growth possible.

EXPLORING THE GOOD LIFE

This chapter will help you think through the process of clarifying your life goals and help you organize a plan of action. Work through each of the exercises carefully.

Finding Out

What is the good life? What would it be like to live the life you most want to live? What would you do? What kind of person would you become? Answer the following questions.

1. What are the ten activities you enjoy the most?

Which of these activities do you do as regularly as you might if you were living the good life? Put a check mark (✔) beside each.

_____

_____

_____

_____

_____

_____

Which of these activities would you really like to include in your long-term career goals? Put a star (★) beside each.

_____

_____

_____

_____

2. What are the five characteristics you most admire in others?

Which of these characteristics do you now have? Put a check mark (✔) beside each.

_____

_____

_____

_____

_____

3. What are the five phrases that best describe the good life for you?

_____

_____

_____

_____

_____

Goal-Exploration Exercises

As you approach the following exercise, avoid seeking security by setting goals that are so easily achieved that they provide no challenge. On the other hand, be as realistic as you can. Do not at this time worry about how you are going to achieve these goals; rather, give yourself free rein to translate your dreams into real goals.

Take three or four minutes to answer each of the questions below. Just make brief notes to yourself—as many as you can in this relatively short time.

21

1. If you learned today that you would die in three months, how would you really want to live until then?

2. What are the most satisfying ways you currently spend your time?

3. How would you like to spend the next four years of your life?

4. What would you really like to achieve in your life? What would you really like to be?

You have spent just a short time on an important task. Now read the answers to yourself. Do you want to add or change anything? Is there any significant part of the total scheme of your life that you have left out? Do your answers include things that are really fun? Do they include involvement with exciting people and exciting tasks?

LISTING LIFE GOALS

Life goals are general statements of where you would like to go with your life—things you would like to achieve, to be, or to do. You might, for example, write: "I would like to become a more loving father and husband" or "I would like to become a truly healthy and vital person." Using your answers to the four questions on page 22, make a list of your life goals. Note that this is just a preliminary list, so write as many goals as you can.

Establishing Priorities

Now you are ready to organize your goals in order of importance.

We can never achieve everything we have dreamed of, so we constantly have to make choices in life. At this point you must make choices as to the few goals that are really important to you. You must concentrate on them, cutting away other goals so that you can grow in a realistic way without frittering away your time or becoming overwhelmed.

Which of your goals are most important to you? Spend some time selecting your **top three goals,** and write them in the following spaces.

Goal A

_____

_____

_____

Goal B

_____

_____

_____

Goal C

_____

_____

_____

Refining Your Goals

Now spend twenty minutes or so thinking about and refining your goals. A simple statement such as, "I would like to become a more loving father and husband" might develop into, "I would like to become a more loving father and husband by spending more time with my wife and children and by really listening to them, involving myself in more creative projects with them, and helping them grow." Try to refine your goals in the space provided below. As you continue to think about your goals, you will see more clearly what they involve and how you can achieve them.

Goal A

_____

_____

_____

Goal B

_____

_____

_____

Goal C

_____

_____

_____

APPRAISING YOUR GOALS

Now that you have stated and refined your three priority goals as clearly as possible, you will want to appraise them for scope and for difficulty. Ask yourself these questions: "Are the goals grand enough to hold my interest, or will I quickly tire of them and will they fail to increase my capability in the future?" "Have I chosen goals that insure failure because they are unrealistic for me?"

Three goals are not many. Ask yourself if working toward these goals will be really satisfying. If your answer is "No," then formulate one more goal, using the same methods you used in formulating the first three.

A Year from Now, Then Two Years

Where would you like to be as regards each of these goals a year from now? How about two years from now? Make a statement to yourself about each of these intermediate goals.

One Year from Now	Two Years from Now
Goal A	
Goal B	
Goal C	

PLANNING ACTIVITIES

Now that you have selected and clarified three important goals, you are ready to plan activities that will help you move toward them. This is the *doing* part of the program. Think about things you can do over the long run as well as things you can do right away.

Brainstorm Activities

List as many activities as you can that will promote the attainment of your goals. Move quickly from one activity to another; do not stop to edit your list as you go along.

Goal A

_____

_____

_____

Goal B

_____

_____

_____

Goal C

_____

_____

_____

Planning Specific Goal A Activities

Think about your Goal A. Look back at the list on page 28. In the space below, write down as many specific activities as you can that will promote that goal over the period of time shown above each column.

Today	This Week	This Month	This Year

Planning Specific Goal B Activities

Think about your Goal B. Look back at the list on page 28. In the space below, write down as many specific activities as you can that will promote that goal over the period of time shown above each column.

Today	This Week	This Month	This Year

Planning Specific Goal C Activities

Think about your Goal C. Look back at the list on page 28. In the space below, write down as many specific activities as you can that will promote that goal over the period of time shown above each column.

Today	This Week	This Month	This Year

Now you have invested yourself in a program for personal growth by specifying your life goals. Check to see if your goals will be satisfying to you and to others who are important to you by examining each for the following:

1. Are they worthy goals? Do they involve things that will be really satisfying in human terms (for example, close relationships with others)? Do they contribute to the welfare of society? Do they carry monetary rewards?

2. Will the process of moving toward the goal be pleasant, rewarding, and fulfilling, or will it be mostly drudgery until it is completed? (Remember: to sustain a long-term effort, you need to find some immediate rewards in what you are doing.)

BUILDING THE SUPPORT YOU NEED

In the process of pursuing your goals, you will need the support of family and friends to help you sustain the effort. You may also need new skills, formal credentials, further education, greater physical conditioning, or particular tools. The final activity of this chapter is listing the kinds of support you will need in your growth program. Imagine yourself actually moving through the next three years as you seek to achieve your goals. What problems will you encounter? What help and tools will you need to progress toward your goals? List them here.

RECOMMENDED READING

Dyer, W. *Your Erroneous Zones.* New York: Funk and Wagnalls, 1976. This volume offers treatment for problems such as being plagued by guilt or worry, being stuck in a job that is not satisfying, or not being able to say "No" to things you do not want and being afraid to go after the things you do. Well written and highly readable, this book presents solutions to problems that would otherwise hinder your personal growth.

Powell, J. *Fully Human, Fully Alive.* Niles, Ill.: Argus, 1976. A very readable book about how our "vision" shapes our lives. The author explains some common misconceptions and some of the sources that create our perceptions of ourselves, others, and the world around us. A key point throughout the book is that improving our self-talk leads to being "fully human, fully alive."

taking command
of your life

Once upon a time a youth named Timothy Green dreamed of becoming an outstanding classical guitarist, playing the works of the great masters with sensitivity and power before admiring audiences throughout the world. His flawless performances would cause people to love him and honor him as a great musician.

Timothy knew that his goal was noble one, and he knew that it was what he really wanted out of life. Although he was told he had musical talent, he never seemed to find time to take music lessons. Something else always got in the way.

As a young man, Timothy was busy with his studies in school. After he came home from school he would rest awhile, then do his chores. After dinner he did his homework, watched TV, or went out with his friends. But Timothy's life was not his own. He still dreamed about the day when he would become a great musician.

Graduation day was an important one for Timothy, because now for the first time in his life he was in control of his own time. He moved out of his parents' home and into a room of his own. He found a job working in a local factory. He liked his job quite well, but it made him so tired that he had no time to devote to his music.

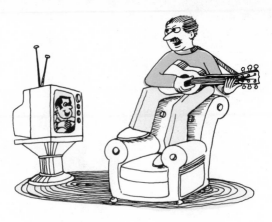

Two years later Timothy married, and soon he and his wife had two children. Although Timothy loved his family, he found himself getting more and more entangled in the day-to-day struggle for survival. He still thought occasionally about his dream of becoming a great musician. He began to tell himself that someday he would study music just for the fun of it; he realized he could no longer become a professional.

One day as Timothy was crossing the street, he was hit by a car. As he lay dying, he thought about his dream. He felt he had been cheated, but he scarcely knew who or what had cheated him. He only knew that he could have been a great musician if he had put his dream first.

■ ■ ■

As we see from the story of Timothy Green, just having dreams is not enough to promote personal growth. In order to realize your goals you must translate them into specific tasks, then find or make time to perform those tasks. Taking charge of your time can be accomplished in roughly four steps:

1. Review how you are currently using your time. Interestingly enough, most people do not know how they use their time. Much of it just slips away.

2. Organize your daily and weekly tasks in order of importance to you. Some tasks have to be done as part of your job or career; others must be done to fulfill responsibilities to family and friends. Some tasks contribute to your growth; others are just a waste of time.

3. Eliminate the tasks that have become unimportant or unproductive for you. Circumstances change continually, and you may find that many activities that were important or worthwhile to you a year ago are no longer so today.

4. Make some time available for your personal growth. This might involve setting aside time for your own meditation and relaxation, for leisure with family and friends, for renewing your skills, for structuring your time, or for doing some creative tasks.

CONTROLLING YOUR OWN TIME

Many people make the mistake of believing that their time is controlled by their family, friends, teachers, or work supervisors. It is true that we often give away our time without much thought, and it is also true that others often have legitimate claims on our time. But you can control a good deal of your own time

simply by spending a few minutes sorting through your commitments and planning more effectively. You can question the demands upon your time and learn to control a greater part of it. If you ask yourself the right questions, you will find that you can be free to be with those you choose and do activities you prefer.

STRUCTURING YOUR TIME

First, ask yourself just how you are using your time. As mentioned earlier, most people have only a vague notion of how they use their time. You may be surprised when you see what you are actually doing with yours.

Second, ask yourself if you choose really important ways of using time. How many of your minutes and hours are pilfered by routine and habitual activities?

Finally, ask yourself which ways of using time help you grow, and which ways hinder you. Which of your weekly activities might you easily dispense with?

DISCOVERING YOUR WEEK

The following exercise will help you answer the questions you just asked yourself. It contains a list of activities in which you might be involved during the week. You may delete or add activities that reflect your own routine. First, rank the activities by importance: most important 1, less important 2, and least important 3. Next, list the total time you spend on each activity each week. Finally, decide whether or not the time spent on that activity contributes to your personal growth. Put a check mark (✔) under the appropriate heading—"Growthful" or "Not Growthful."

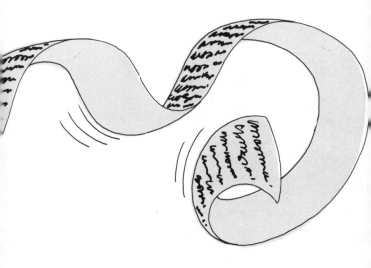

Work Activities	Rank	Time Spent	Growthful	Not Growthful
Planning work projects				
Performing on the job				
Taking breaks				
Recuperating from work				
Thinking about work during off hours				
(Add others here.)				
_____				
_____				
_____				
_____				
Socializing Activities				
Being with spouse				
Being with children				
Being with entire family				
Being with friends by yourself				
Being with friends and spouse				
Being with friends and family				
(Add others here.)				
_____				
_____				
_____				

Recreational Activities	Rank	Time Spent	Growthful	Not Growthful
Reading				
Engaging in sports				
Watching TV				
Conversing				
Attending parties				
Being by yourself				
(Add others here.)				
_____				
_____				
_____				
_____				
Religious Activities				
Political Activities				
Community Activities				
(Add others here.)				
_____				
_____				
_____				
_____				
_____				
_____				

Planning Your Week

Some of your time is bound up in routine activities. You go to work or school, or manage a household. Most of us believe that we "must do" at least these things and probably a lot more. But that list of "must do" activities can get out of hand very quickly if you are not careful. How can you get it under control? Look at each of your "must dos." How many of them are things you choose to do? How many are you doing out of habit? As you eliminate the unnecessary "must do" tasks, you free your time for more important things.

Take a few minutes to make a list of all the things that you feel you "must do."

_____

_____

_____

_____

_____

_____

_____

_____

_____

_____

Now ask yourself if any of these items can be eliminated.	Can effective planning reduce the amount of time spent on the "must do" items?

Your job, your schooling, and your relationships with family and friends all thrust responsibilities upon you—responsibilities which structure your time. That time can be personally rewarding if well planned. However, most of us need more "personal" time.

You will not reach your goals through automatic or routine behavior. You must learn to manage your time so as to release yourself from the things you "must do" each day in order to be able to do those things that you would really like to do for pleasure or for the realization of your life goals.

How can you use your time more effectively? Executives and other busy people have found it helpful to make a list of the things that really need to be done each day. The worksheet on page 44 has a column on the left entitled, "To Do Today." Think carefully about the next twenty-four hours and make a list of "To Do Today" items in the left column—all the things you feel you must do during the day. Do not worry about organizing them at this point.

To Do Today	Rank	Plans

You will probably find that you have a long list. If you are like most people, you have a backlog of unfinished business—things you have been putting off. Do not be discouraged by that. Once you have cleaned up that backlog, you can move on to your life goals more assertively.

Now that you have a list of things you would like to accomplish today, pick out the most important of those—the ones that *must* be done today—and put an A opposite them in the column entitled "Rank." Next, select the items that are important but need not be done today. Put a B opposite them. All remaining items will be C items—those that can be done in the distant future or can be eliminated entirely. The last column is marked "Plans" to help you note what you can do to accomplish each task and when you intend to do it.

In the previous chapter you established the important goals in your life. Personal growth means not only establishing goals but working toward their fulfillment. This can be done only by accomplishing something each day, however small, that contributes to achieving them. So be sure your "To Do Today" items include things that will contribute to your personal growth.

The following pages contain a sample weekly and daily planner. Practice planning your time for the next week.

Planning for the Week Ahead

In the boxes below, jot down the tasks you are responsible for or would otherwise like to accomplish this week.

Monday

Tuesday

Wednesday

Thursday

Friday

Saturday

Sunday

Daily Planning Sheet		
To Do Today	**Rank**	**Plans**
Growth Projects Today		

Daily Planning Sheet		
To Do Today	**Rank**	**Plans**
Growth Projects Today		

Daily Planning Sheet		
To Do Today	**Rank**	**Plans**
Growth Projects Today		

Daily Planning Sheet		
To Do Today	**Rank**	**Plans**
Growth Projects Today		

Daily Planning Sheet		
To Do Today	**Rank**	**Plans**
Growth Projects Today		

Daily Planning Sheet		
To Do Today	Rank	Plans
Growth Projects Today		

Daily Planning Sheet

To Do Today	Rank	Plans
Growth Projects Today		

RECOMMENDED READING

Ellis, A., and Harper, R. A. *A New Guide to Rational Living*. Hollywood, Calif.: Wilshire Book, 1975. The authors discuss the link between feelings and beliefs, ways to think ourselves out of emotional upsets, and how to accept reality, control our own destinies, become creative, and live rationally. This readable book is now basic in cognitive therapy.

Goble, G. *The Third Force*. New York: Pocket Books, 1970. The author presents the psychology of Abraham Maslow in a highly readable and interesting way and does an excellent job of showing the organized unity of Maslow's thought. In presenting the basic theory of human potential, this book has become basic reading in the psychology of the healthy person.

building confidence by recognizing success

As was pointed out in the first chapter, we all have an image of ourselves that we use as a point of reference in our feelings and behavior. If we see ourselves as competent and able to do things, we feel confident and take psychological risks. If, on the other hand, we see ourselves as incompetent, we lack confidence and feel threatened by new tasks and situations.

In a practical sense, your self-concept is the answer you give yourself when you ask general questions such as, "Can I succeed in this new career?" or, "Is it reasonable to think of myself as socially popular?" If you generally answer yes to such questions, you have a good self-concept. If you generally answer no or, "I don't think I can do that," you have a poor self-concept. Your answers are linked with your feelings. "Yes" answers indicate feelings of optimism and courage. "No" answers are self-defeating statements that lead to pessimism and feelings of incompetence.

Your self-concept is a complex thing—a creature of several forces, some of which are easily recognizable. Simply put, your self-concept is formed by the messages you receive from the significant people in your life and by the experiences you had as a child. As you grow older, you forget the early messages and experiences; your self-concept is maintained by the things

55

you continually tell yourself in your self-talk and by the selective perceptions you make of your experiences. But you can change your self-concept by making more adventurous decisions and by giving yourself credit for the successes you do experience.

You can rebuild your self-concept in increasingly positive ways by persistently observing these injunctions:

1. Explore your self-concept and dismiss the negative messages you received as a child.
2. Take some chances and avoid always playing it safe, by choosing some psychological risks and some adventures.
3. Credit yourself for your efforts and for the successes that you do experience in your life.
4. Change the tone of your self-talk to positive, self-supportive statements.

EXPLORING YOUR SELF-CONCEPT

Early in your life people sent you messages about your worth, your competence, your appearance, and your role in life; in short, they told you who you were. If they sent good and powerful messages, you probably developed a positive self-concept. For example, if your parents told you that you were bright, friendly, nice to be around, dependable, and loyal, you probably built a very positive self-concept. That allowed you to start the process of personal growth early because you tended to be curious, exploratory, and relatively unafraid of the world and other people. Most of us, however, do not get consistently positive messages from the people around us. They may tell us we are bright or friendly, but they also tell us we make too many mistakes and act childishly. Too often we take these messages that were sent only to correct our behavior as statements about our worth as a person.

The messages that the significant people in your life give you are starting points of your self-concept and act as predictors of your behavior and of your success or failure as a person. This sets in motion a style of behavior that, in turn, reinforces that self-concept. For example, if your mother told you that you were just like her because she, too, had trouble with arithmetic, then you probably tended to do poorly in arithmetic, reinforcing her prediction. Her prediction contributed to your behavior, and your behavior reinforced her prediction.

Use the exercise on pages 58 and 60 to explore the early influences that contributed to your current self-concept. Take ten to fifteen minutes to answer the questions by recalling some of the messages the significant people in your life gave you.

Think about parents and other important adults in your early life.

What did they say about your lovableness?

_____

_____

_____

What did they say about your physical appearance?

_____

_____

_____

What did they say about your intelligence?

_____

_____

_____

What did they say about your general ability?

_____

_____

_____

What predictions did they make about your future?

_____

_____

_____

How did they compare you with other children?

_____

_____

_____

Think about your teachers and childhood friends.
What did your teachers tell you about your intelligence?

_____

_____

_____

What did they tell you about your physical skills?

_____

_____

_____

What message did school friends give you about your general worth as a person?

_____

_____

_____

Did your teachers or peers give you a nickname? What did it mean to you?

_____

_____

_____

The important thing to note is that much of what you were told as a child either occurred during moments of stress or was intended to be a casual statement made for no particular reason. Your parents often said things about you when they were angry or upset; your teachers said things when they were disappointed; your peers said things just to tease you or try to appear important. Some of the messages were posi-

tive, growthful messages, but many were not. Once you have explored those early formative messages, you can begin to dismiss those that are destructive.

Although your early experiences contributed to the formation of your self-concept, they probably happened in a random way at first. Your successes might have occurred because you were competent and healthy or because you had been prepared for success by older brothers and sisters. Your failures, too, might have been accidental. Whatever the case, success and failure are important. When you are successful, you think the world is beautiful, and you are proud of yourself. When you fail, you conclude that you have little power over things and that you must fight the world to protect yourself.

We all try to interpret our experiences and make sense of them. For instance, one person at work gets criticized and says inwardly, "I'm a dummy" or "It's not my fault; people are just picking on me." Another person says, "I made a mistake that I won't make again" or "I've learned something from that." Our interpretation of what happens is at least as important as what actually happens; and we can control the inter-

61

pretation even when we cannot control the event. Our self-talk is the key to the tone of our interpretation.

Can you think of two or three experiences in your early life that helped you develop the positive side of your self-concept? Spend a few minutes thinking about those good experiences. Jot them down here.

Can you think of two or three early experiences that caused you to develop the negative side of your self-concept? What did you tell yourself about these experiences? Write it down here.

As you look back on those experiences, can you now see that you were not really so bad and that you could have interpreted the experiences more positively?

MAINTAINING AND CHANGING YOUR SELF-CONCEPT

Now that you have begun to think about self-concept, you need to ask yourself: "How and why do I maintain a poor self-concept after I have recognized it and decided to change it?"

You maintain a poor self-concept in two important ways—by negative self-talk and by selective perception that puts you down.

Negative self-talk is a kind of demeaning internal discussion you have with yourself when you are discouraged. You tell yourself such things as, "Gee, I'm really dumb" or "I'm no good at this" or "I don't think I will ever get ahead." Sometimes self-talk is an automatic response to what other people have told you about yourself; other times it is consciously thought out. The tone of your self-talk is crucial in maintaining or changing your self-concept.

Take a few minutes to check out your self-talk. What do you tell yourself in these situations?

When you are criticized by someone:

_____

_____

_____

When you do something really good for a friend:

_____

_____

_____

When you are trying some new skill, such as typing or skiing, and have not yet mastered it:

_____

_____

_____

When you think about meeting new people:

_____

_____

_____

When you are not as attractive as you would like to be:

_____

_____

_____

Does your self-talk help you feel strong, competent, and successful, or does it make you feel frustrated and unhappy? If it makes you feel bad, turn it around. People often think that they are "just telling themselves the truth" when they think of themselves as powerless, unworthy, and incompetent. But that kind of statement fails to consider a great truth: "I can grow and learn and become the person I want to be if I am persistent." Everything can change.

The second element in maintaining a poor self-concept is your selective perception. You take into account and register only part of your experience. If you notice and internalize only the negative aspects of your life, you will maintain a negative self-concept. However, if you use selective perception to pinpoint the positive aspects of your life, you can build a more powerful self-concept and change your whole attitude about yourself.

BUILDING A SUCCESS JOURNAL

One way to change your negative self-talk and selective perception is to develop a Success Journal. Begin to structure your time by making a "To Do Today" list as you did in chapter 3. At the end of each day, review your successes by listing them in your Success Journal.

Use the following exercises to practice keeping a Success Journal.

To Do Today	Rank	Commitments

Success Journal

List all the things you accomplished today from your "To Do Today" list.

To Do Today	Rank	Commitments

Success Journal

List all the things you accomplished today. Be sure to credit yourself for the times you made an effort to achieve a goal even though you failed.

To Do Today	Rank	Commitments

Success Journal

List all the things you accomplished today. Have you been working on your most important life goals? Plan something for tomorrow that will contribute to one of your growth goals.

To Do Today	Rank	Commitments

Success Journal

List all the things you accomplished today. Did you do something for yourself?

To Do Today	Rank	Commitments

Success Journal

List all the things you accomplished today. Have you been able to eliminate some of your "To Do Today" items?
If so, do you feel good about it? Check your "To Do Today" list for routine items that might be eliminated.

To Do Today	Rank	Commitments

Success Journal

List all the things you accomplished today. Have you been saying positive things about yourself? Be persistent in your positive self-talk. Read your Success Journal to yourself after you have completed it.

RECOMMENDED READING

Lembo, J. *Help Yourself*. Niles, Ill.: Argus, 1974. A well-written document that deals with the meaning of personal relationships, relationships with the environment, the development of personal goals, and the importance of personal thought. Thoughts, the author claims, can lead to greater self-acceptance and mistakes can lead to greater learning.

Smith, M. J. *When I Say No, I Feel Guilty*. New York: Bantam, 1975. The author deals with the idea of assertiveness in clear and lucid prose. He outlines a number of assertiveness skills and shows, through sample dialogues, how they are applied.

self-assessment, growth projects, and beliefs

An interesting phenomenon in American culture is the strong bias against a person's planning for success. This attitude appears to be the result of three powerful influences. One influence may have been that of a religious tradition that taught you to avoid thinking about yourself because you might commit the "sin" of pride. Your religious training may have given you the feeling that to want the best for yourself is selfish; a more honorable goal is to surrender your life to others. A second influence was your home. As a youngster you may have been told that you should not "show off." Thus you may have thought your parents were telling you that you should not enjoy yourself or be so pleased with yourself. Finally, school undoubtedly had its impact on you through your classmates. Your friends may have been suspicious if you projected success for yourself. They may have felt it was wrong for you to admit you expected to do well on a test, take first place in a contest, or be chosen for some honor.

How can those influences affect your goals and plans for successful living? For one thing, they can set a strong foundation for "holding back," for refusing to think about what you expect and want in life. You, like many others, may have learned early to set limitations on your potential—on your success, efficiency, and

sociability. Most of us develop only about ten percent of our capability. We are not nearly so limited as we have been led or have led ourselves to believe.

The bias against planning for success can keep you from talking about success for yourself because others would disapprove or because it would seem "sinful." From there it is an easy step to decide that you should probably not even think about succeeding. But how can you move toward success until you have envisioned it?

The notion of intentionally setting out to learn something about themselves makes some people feel uncomfortable. Even people who are otherwise rational feel that setting up a project for personal growth is too "mechanical" or " inauthentic." Forget that! Remember, you have a constitutionally guaranteed right to pursue happiness. Intentional growth projects can accomplish a dramatic change in you by turning weaknesses into strengths. A small change can lead to larger ones by creating a spirit of optimism and adventure.

Your self-imposed limitations are a nuisance, but they can be overcome with a little determination once you have learned the appropriate skills. The rest of this chapter will help you develop those skills. Complete the exercise below, "Looking at Yourself." Then practice the skills of planning personal growth projects and building them through the necessary six steps.

LOOKING AT YOURSELF

Each of the questions below has under it two words or phrases connected by a line, representing opposite extremes of response to that question. Your answer probably lies somewhere between the two extremes. Put a circle on each line where you think you fall on the continuum between the extremes, and a triangle on each line where you think you would like to be. This is known as self-assessment.

1. Can you imagine yourself highly successful in some important dimension of your life where you are not now successful?

not at all   *easily can*

2. Do you travel as much as you would like to do?

little travel   *much travel*

3. Are you as creative and expressive as you would like to be?

_____
uncreative   very creative

4. Are you as skilled, healthy, and attractive as you would like to be?

_____
not at all   very much so

5. Do you have the skills to make new friends and to relate intimately with your current friends?

_____
socially unskilled   socially skilled

6. Does your work nourish your social and psychological growth?

_____
unfulfilling   satisfying

7. Do you have a clear view of your life goals?

_____
unclear   very clear

8. Can you be as open and affectionate as you would like to be?

_____
inhibited   spontaneous

9. Can you say "No" to people, when appropriate, without guilt feelings?

_____
very guilty   secure

10. Can you take on new challenges with a sense of confidence?

_____

unconfident   *very confident*

11. Can you relax away your tensions when appropriate?

_____

uptight   *easily relaxed*

12. Can you dismiss old and lingering feelings such as guilt and disappointment? Can you forgive yourself for mistakes?

_____

not at all   *easily*

PLANNING A GROWTH PROJECT

Now that you have assessed some of your desires for personal growth, you are ready to think about growth projects in a more specific way. It may be helpful to plan them in four steps or stages:
1. Recognize and choose a general area of growth.
2. Make more specific plans. This means sharpening the focus of your goal, reviewing the means available for achieving it, and building a support system to help you achieve it.
3. Carry out the project. This means practicing— renewing friendships by calling an acquaintance on the telephone or seeking out someone you do not know and striking up a conversation.
4. Acknowledge your efforts. Do not lose the full benefit of your growth adventures by failing to note successes. The Success Journal is an important tool for this last step.

Personal growth projects can be long-term things (such as losing twenty-five pounds) or smaller, but still significant things (such as asking a friend to go to the movies, jogging a mile this afternoon, writing a letter you have been putting off, or simply reading a book for recreation). The value of a growth project is measured not so much by the time involved as by the significance of the growth experience. Do the following exercise to practice being specific about planning and building a growth project.

1. Look back at the twelve self-assessment questions on pages 75-77 and choose one to represent an area of growth for yourself. Write it here in brief form.

   _____

   _____

   _____

2. Sharpen the focus of the project by stating a specific goal. If your area of growth is interpersonal relationships, you may have a goal of joining a club to make new friends or sitting down to clear up a misunderstanding with a family member or friend. State your goal here. _____

   _____

   _____

3. What means do you have available to you? What people, agencies, tools, or other skills might help you reach the goal? Take a minute to assess the means available and note them here. _____

   _____

   _____

4. What forces might keep you from succeeding in your efforts? How can you enhance your chances of success? _____

   _____

   _____

5. When and where will you carry out the project? Write it down here. _____

_____

_____

Take a few minutes, relax, and imagine yourself being successful.

6. After you have planned and carried out the project, acknowledge your efforts by writing a report of your efforts to yourself. _____

_____

_____

These steps can be applied to any of the items from the "Looking at Yourself" activity or to any project you pick that might result in your personal growth. Remember, the more you choose to expand your boundaries and develop your potential, the more you have to offer others and society.

CREATING A NEW WORLD

We all live in a world of our own creation. None of us has been everywhere or seen everything, but we still shape our world by "filling in the blanks" of our experience with our beliefs, creating personal images of and building reliable predictions about the people and things around us, and making judgments about what is good or bad, safe or dangerous in our world.

So we plan, feel, and respond more to our experiences and our beliefs than we do to the real world. Our beliefs are the key to both our feelings and our behaviors. Since we create our own beliefs, we also create our own feelings and behaviors. And what we have created, we can recreate. That is why we can grow. Our beliefs are exciting areas to explore.

There was a time when professional mental-health workers did not understand the connections between the things we believe and the way we feel and act. Thanks to the work of people like Albert Ellis, psychologists have come to understand the link between beliefs, patterns of emotional life, and behaviors. Ellis found that there are certain destructive, irrational beliefs that, when held, cause unwanted patterns of feeling. For example, if you think that it is vitally important to be accepted by all of the people in your life all of the time, you will be dependent rather than interdependent, other-directed rather than inner-directed. You will waste your energy by always trying to anticipate other people's responses, striving to please others all the time, and having to deal with hurt feelings when you are criticized or rejected. On the other hand, if you are rational, you not only cherish others' comments and ideas but your own as well. Consequently, you can be much more creative and resourceful.

While irrational beliefs cause problems and block personal growth, rational or positive beliefs help us interpret our world in ways that will promote a healthy emotional life and contribute to the adventure of personal growth. They also help us relate to other people in positive, friendly ways.

GROWTH-PRODUCING BELIEFS

The following seven statements represent rational, positive beliefs that you will want to build into your own belief system:

1. My self-acceptance and growth are best fostered by realizing that I have both the right and the power to be self-directed, to make my own decisions and maintain my own feelings.

2. My highest level of self-fulfillment is realized through my connectedness with others.

3. I have a reservoir of strength which allows me to meet life's challenges in various ways, and many of the ways I might choose will add to my personal growth.

4. Taking time to deal with problems enhances my psychological strength and affords me more time to grow.

5. I am at my best when I live in the present and plan for, rather than dread, the future; when I derive

strength and pleasure, rather than guilt, from the past.

6. My growth is best promoted by recognizing my connectedness with my environment.

7. I maximize my growth by learning, doing, and creating as well as by profiting from my mistakes, cherishing my successes, and having a willingness to make growth decisions.

The following chapters examine these growth-producing beliefs and provide exercises to help build them into your belief system.

RECOMMENDED READING

Cordell, F., and Giebler, G. *Psychological War on Fat.* Niles, Ill.: Argus, 1977. The primary focus of this book is the attainment of permanent weight loss and improved physical health. Additional benefits occur as the reader learns to build a positive self-image, let go of unwanted feelings, and dispute destructive self-talk. The reader is also challenged to develop creativity and to practice using psychological tools to change his or her thoughts and feelings into assets that provide a stimulating life.

Greenwald, J. *Be the Person You Were Meant to Be.* New York: Dell, 1973. A highly readable and enjoyable self-help book about how we spend our time, get ourselves trapped in destructive life-styles, and experience loneliness due to an inability to develop good relating skills. The author points out troublesome behavior and offers means for solving problems encountered in living.

Krishnamurti, J. *You Are the World.* New York: Harper & Row, 1972. Problems the world over are similar. They include establishing freedom, curbing violence, bringing about better relationships between people, showing decency to others in the face of constant conflict, and trying to live in peace with one-self and one's neighbors. The primary theme of Krishnamurti's message is that we cannot begin to solve the world's problems until we come to be at peace with these issues within ourselves.

Maultsby, M. D., *Help Yourself to Happiness Through Rational Self-Counseling.* Boston: Herman Publishing, 1975. Maultsby shows the reader how to pursue personal happiness at his or her own pace. He helps the reader build self-mastery over unwanted feelings by showing how one can learn and practice rational self-help techniques to achieve life goals.

Maultsby, M. D., and Hendricks, A. *You and Your Emotions.* Lexington, Ky.: Univ. of Kentucky Medical Center, 1974. The authors provide cartoon illustrations of the basic emotional self-help principles and techniques used to encourage people to clean up their "internal dialogues." By offering shrewd insights into our unwanted emotions, the book shows what we can do to change them.

self-acceptance

The first growth-producing belief is: "My self-acceptance and growth are best fostered by realizing that I have both the right and the power to be self-directed, to make my own decisions and maintain my own feelings." Many of us believe that we are good only when we win the constant approval of those who are important to us, and that if we lose that approval, something bad will happen. We ride a jolting roller coaster of feeling from joy when accepted to self-hate when rejected. Furthermore, we create the problem of having to act in different ways to please different people.

While it is a beautiful thing to act in ways that please your friends and loved ones, you cannot *always* please them. You make mistakes. Other people do not always understand all the forces acting in your life; they make casual observations and judgments about you. If you take those judgments too seriously, you are voluntarily jumping onto that roller coaster of feelings. In extreme cases you may wind up being totally dependent upon receiving signs of acceptance from other people and feeling desolate when you do not get them.

If you can learn to trust your social and moral judgments, you will shed the unhealthy part of your interactions with others and the need to act in conflicting ways to please them. You will also shed your inner conflict and gain greater peace with yourself.

The following pages are designed to help you explore your beliefs about self-acceptance and build a personal growth project to become more self-accepting. The worksheets on these pages may be used as a journal or completed all at once. If you feel competent in self-acceptance, move on to the next chapter.

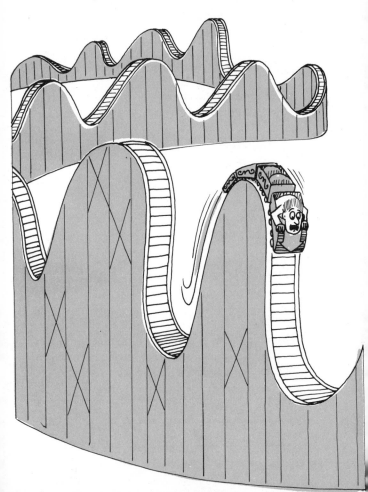

EXPLORING YOUR BELIEFS

Your first task is to get in touch with your beliefs about self-acceptance. Spend ten minutes exploring them, writing down what you really believe. Answer the following questions.

1. After you have completed some important project, how do you feel when others fail to mention it to you? _____

   _____

   _____

   _____

2. How do you feel when others make negative comments or criticisms about your work? _____

   _____

   _____

   _____

3. If you abandon your ideals, goals, and values in order to gain acceptance, how do you feel?

   _____

   _____

   _____

4. How long does it take you to recover your self-acceptance after you have been criticized or rejected by a friend? _____

   _____

   _____

   _____

SUCCESS FANTASY

Your next task is to spend ten minutes imagining yourself in some characteristically troublesome situation and writing about it.

1. Who are the significant people in your life (family, friends, teachers, co-workers, supervisors)? Name them. _____

   _____

   _____

   _____

2. What kinds of situations cause you to fear rejection by these people? _____

   _____

   _____

   _____

3. Think of three specific situations you might face in the near future in which you could temporarily lose the acceptance of one or more of these people. List the situations. _____

   _____

   _____

   _____

4. Imagine each of these situations as vividly as you can, and move through each situation step by step. Now imagine resolving the potential conflict as positively as possible. Imagine yourself being successful and accepted, not rejected.

DISPUTING UNWANTED BELIEFS

Practice disputing your unwanted or irrational beliefs about self-acceptance by moving through the following steps.

1. Think of a recent situation where you felt rejected or criticized by a person significant to you, and recall your feelings. Were you anxious, angry, frightened, or depressed? Briefly describe the situation and how you felt. _____

_____

_____

_____

_____

_____

2. Recall and write down the things you told yourself when you felt rejected. Did you tell yourself negative things such as, "I have finally been caught" or "Now people will really know the true me and something horrible is going to happen"? Did you tell yourself any positive things? As best you can, try to recall what you said to yourself.

_____

_____

_____

_____

_____

3. Are there more positive or powerful things you might have said about yourself and the rejection that would have aided or enhanced your ability to handle the situation successfully? (You might have told yourself, "I have the right to be self-

directed" or you might have repeated the growth-producing belief about self-acceptance.

_____

_____

_____

_____

_____

If you choose to believe that you are always to blame when you are rejected and that your life is ruined as a result of it, you will feel terrible. But if you choose to see yourself as strong and inner-directed, you can handle any situation.

BUILDING A GROWTH PROJECT

A growth project is an intentionally planned experience to help you turn your stumbling blocks into stepping-stones. First, identify some skill, disposition, belief, or relationship you would like to build or change, then plan an experience that will help you do so with the least chance of failure. Second, try as hard as you can to carry out the plan. Finally, run through the experience in your mind and acknowledge your success and growth by asking yourself what new skills, dis-

positions, beliefs, or relationships you created by that experience.

In this experience, self-acceptance, or self-validation, is the skill or disposition you will be seeking. Outline a situation that can be turned into a growth project—one in which you risk rejection and have a chance to face it and grow from the challenge. Cleaning up unfinished business might be one such situation. Others might include reaching out for friendship to someone you are attracted to, proposing a new idea or project at work, expressing either positive or negative feelings toward someone. All such situations can be turned into growth projects.

1. Outline your situation. _____

_____

_____

_____

_____

_____

2. What are the goals of your growth project? (For example: "I would like to gain experience in making friends without fear of rejection.")

_____

_____

_____

_____

_____

3. What support can you build into the project? (For example: help of family or friends, new skills, diet or exercise.) _____

_____

_____

_____

_____

_____

_____

4. What are the likely stumbling blocks in this project? _____

_____

_____

_____

Now take a few minutes to run through the project in your mind, imagining success as you do it.

5. After you have planned and carried out the growth experience, ask yourself what you have learned about yourself: "What new skills and competencies have I gained?" _____

_____

_____

_____

SUCCESS JOURNAL

The following pages contain a journal that will help you explore your beliefs about self-acceptance. Do one section of the journal each day for the next seven days.

To Do Today	Rank	Commitments

Success Journal

Rewrite the following belief in a way that has special meaning to you, and repeat it to yourself during the week: "My self-acceptance and growth are best fostered by realizing that I have both the right and the power to be self-directed, to make my own decisions and maintain my own feelings."

To Do Today	Rank	Commitments

Success Journal

Peace comes with self-acceptance. Jot down something that you have done well and that you feel good about. Give yourself credit for the time, effort, and motivation it took.

To Do Today	Rank	Commitments

Success Journal

Beliefs are reinforced by self-talk. Can you think of times when you tell yourself something about your self-acceptance? Now tell yourself something positive, or repeat your rewritten belief.

To Do Today	Rank	Commitments

Success Journal

When you failed to get the approval of a significant person in your life, was it really so bad? Did it involve exercising some strength of character?

To Do Today	Rank	Commitments

Success Journal

You will have more to offer family and friends when you
have confidence and high self-esteem. Think about
one area of your life where you feel confident. What does
that mean to others in your life?

To Do Today	Rank	Commitments

Success Journal

Build a growth project for yourself. Do something that will really please you and at the same time contribute to others.

To Do Today	Rank	Commitments

Success Journal

Think back through the week. Jot down your successes.
Think of what you have learned about yourself and about
self-acceptance.

RECOMMENDED READING

Benjamin, H. *Basic Self-Knowledge.* New York: Weiser, 1971. Benjamin identifies stumbling blocks to our self-awareness. He shows how we fail to learn from our mistakes because we expend energy in self-justification. Practice in self-observation, he contends, will enable us to know ourselves, accept ourselves, and learn from our errors.

Dass, R. *The Only Dance There Is.* Garden City, N.Y.: Anchor Press/Doubleday, 1974. This book looks at the nature of the universe, human consciousness, and the harmonious flow that can exist between the two. It offers the reader a new perspective on life—that it is precious and need not be a constant struggle; that learning from the laws of nature is a special way to appreciate how best to spend your life flowing downstream rather than swimming upstream.

Phillips, P., and Cordell, F. *Am I OK?* Niles, Ill.: Argus, 1975. The authors focus upon people's OKness by facilitating the reader's awareness of each person's inherent potential. They help the reader understand how to move in a positive direction by looking at how to use time, relate to others, and contribute to the well-being of self and others.

friendships

No one doubts that personal relationships are important to personal growth. Abraham Maslow went so far as to ask if any of us can approach self-actualization without feeling deeply loved by another person. This leads to the second growth-producing belief: "My highest level of self-fulfillment is realized through my connectedness with others."

> In positive friendly relationships, people share themselves and their feelings; as a result, they bridge the chasm between themselves and others. In close relationships, conflict, distrust, negative feelings, and negative beliefs about the world fade. Closeness frees energy and allows people to live fully human lives and to feel, listen, trust, choose, respond, and create. It is through positive friendly relationships that people gain the emotional strength to be truly helping people. Such relationships involve a direct, honest, satisfying, and intense sharing between two or more people. In a friendly relationship, there is no exploitation or manipulation.*

*Paul L. Phillips and Franklin D. Cordell, *Am I OK?* (Niles, Ill.: Argus, 1975), p. 44.

Our relationships with other people can facilitate or hinder our personal growth. We can relate to people in close, intimate ways so that we are stimulated and motivated to grow and enhance our well-being, or we can relate to people in painful and deadening ways. A positive relationship is something we continually build but never really complete. The important thing is to build our relationships consciously, with mutual growth in mind.

LOOKING AT YOUR RELATIONSHIPS

Imagine yourself at the center of the diagram below, and put the names of three people who are highly significant to you on the lines attached to each spoke. Select especially significant people, ones you would like to build a more positive, intimate, or ongoing relationship with.

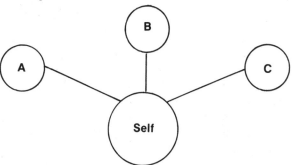

The ideal relationship is mutually satisfying, stimulating, and growth-producing; it is characterized by mutual trust and is self-correcting.

101

Satisfaction

The first question to ask yourself is: What are the important elements of an effective relationship? At the highest level is a mutually satisfying relationship of love, in which you freely express yourself to your partner and receive some basic satisfaction of your social needs. In a work environment, a satisfying relationship might mean mutually contributing to each other's creative efforts or helping each other achieve goals.

Check out your relationships to see if they are mutually satisfying. Be sure to look at the "mutual" as well as the "satisfying" aspects of the relationship.

Refer back to the diagram on page 101 and answer the following questions about the significant individuals whom you named.

Relationship A
What are you doing to please this person and what are you receiving in your relationship with this person?

_____

_____

_____

What can you do to improve this dimension of the relationship? _____

_____

_____

Relationship B
What are you doing to please this person and what are you receiving in your relationship with this person?

_____

_____

_____

What can you do to improve this dimension of the relationship? _____

_____

_____

Relationship C
What are you doing to please this person and what are you receiving in your relationship with this person?

_____

_____

_____

What can you do to improve this dimension of the relationship? _____

_____

_____

Stimulation

An effective relationship needs to be stimulating, interesting, and exciting at least part of the time. A love relationship is always exciting, but even people in love tend to drift apart at times. The sought-after relationship is one in which partners fight against that drift and punctuate the relationship with stimulating and exciting moments. When a relationship stagnates, it stops contributing to personal growth.

Relationship A
Is this person interesting to you? Are you interesting to this person? _____

_____

_____

What might you do to make this relationship more interesting? _____

_____

_____

Relationship B
Is this person interesting to you? Are you interesting to
this person?_____

_____

_____

What might you do to make this relationship more
interesting? _____

_____

_____

Relationship C
Is this person interesting to you? Are you interesting to
this person?_____

_____

_____

What might you do to make this relationship more
interesting? _____

_____

_____

Growth Production

The ideal relationship should be mutually
growth-producing in some way, conducted so that both
parties learn things about themselves, about their
relationship, and about each other. This requires a kind
of openness with a critical, but supportive, dimension.

Relationship A
How have both of you grown as a result of this
relationship? _____

_____

_____

_____

What might you do to make this a more growth-
producing relationship?_____

_____

Relationship B
How have both of you grown as a result of this
relationship? _____

_____

_____

What might you do to make this a more growth-
producing relationship?_____

_____

Relationship C
How have both of you grown as a result of this
relationship? _____

_____

_____

_____

What might you do to make this a more growth-
producing relationship?_____

_____

Trust

Finally, the best relationships are ones based on trust.
Trust is linked directly with feelings of security.
Your ability to stretch your boundaries is related to your
level of confidence. Trust produces confidence and is
something to be sought after in a relationship.

When you have a relationship with people whom you feel you cannot trust, you usually find that the relationship is not growth-producing.

Relationship A
What in this relationship furthers or inhibits mutual trust? _____

_____

_____

What might you do to be more trusting and trust-worthy?_____

_____

_____

_____

Relationship B
What in this relationship furthers or inhibits mutual trust? _____

_____

_____

What might you do to be more trusting and trust-worthy?_____

_____

_____

_____

Relationship C
What in this relationship furthers or inhibits mutual trust? _____

_____

_____

106

What might you do to be more trusting and trust-worthy?_____

_____

_____

_____

SELF-CORRECTING RELATIONSHIPS

The foundation of an effective relationship is communication—open and honest communication that builds trust and growth, rather than ulterior and manipulative communication. A relationship is self-correcting only when you and the other person honestly and assertively express your needs and wants and when you both talk intimately about your feelings and your dreams. When you or your partner try to manipulate one another by using ulterior communication, you will find that the relationship is not need-fulfilling.

The communication process in any relationship should help people accept themselves and others at a very basic level. You need to communicate understanding, trust, and affection in order to build a sense of confidence and power. When you find it difficult to talk about feelings and needs, you have trouble accepting others. Then distrust creeps in.

A relationship is intimate when you and your partner talk about your feelings and about things that are happening now. Your relationship becomes more intimate when you talk about important things rather than trivial things.

SUCCESS JOURNAL

The next few pages contain a journal to be used over a seven-day period. Use this to explore your understanding of relationships.

To Do Today	Rank	Commitments

Success Journal

All of us want to be recognized in a positive way, but many of us do not know how to ask for that recognition. Can you think of a good way to ask for recognition that will enhance your relationship with others?

To Do Today	Rank	Commitments

Success Journal

"My highest level of self-fulfillment is realized through my connectedness with others." Think about what that belief means in your life, and repeat it to yourself during the week.

To Do Today	Rank	Commitments

Success Journal

Self-disclosure is the skill of tactfully and honestly communicating your feelings, needs, and expectations to another person. It often takes courage. It is the first step in building a positive, intimate relationship. How have you practiced self-disclosure today?

To Do Today	Rank	Commitments

Success Journal

Whom are you helping to grow? How are you doing it?
Think about all the things you have done that help others.

To Do Today	Rank	Commitments

Success Journal

Are there people around you whom you would like to know better? Make plans to meet someone new or to get to know someone more intimately.

To Do Today	Rank	Commitments

Success Journal

Do you know how to give positive, supportive recognition to the important people in your life? Practice some phrases that convey your feelings and appreciation of others.

To Do Today	Rank	Commitments

Success Journal

We are nurtured by the support and recognition other people give us. Can you accept support and recognition, internalize them, and use them for your personal growth? What have you done with the support or recognition others gave you today?

RECOMMENDED READING

Fromm, E. *The Art of Loving*. New York: Harper & Row, 1956. Fromm discusses the meaning of love and how it offers a solution to the problems of being human beings in search of meaning. He differentiates between brotherly love, motherly love, erotic love, self-love, and the love of God. After his commentary on the disintegration of Western peoples who sell themselves for the attainment of material goods, he concludes with an antidote to such self-disintegration, i.e., practicing the art of loving.

Simon, S. *Caring, Feeling, Touching*. Niles, Ill.: Argus, 1976. The pleasures of being sensuous human beings are highlighted in this artful and descriptive narrative. Simon underscores the importance of physical touch administered with love and caring. Touching, feeling, and caring are specific ways of allowing others to enrich your life and giving others support in their growth.

115

your reservoir of strength

Fairness and justice are major themes in American society. They are worthy and respectable goals. However, we live in a less-than-perfect society where we are treated unfairly at times and where even the people closest to us are not always as kind, just, and fair to us as we would want. Although that is a grim statement, it can lead to some very beneficial results if we learn to understand and accept it. This brings us to our third growth-producing belief: "I have a reservoir of strength which allows me to meet life's challenges in various ways, and many of the ways I might choose will add to my personal growth."

Many people have become great and have made significant contributions to family, friends, and country in the face of personal adversities. You can do the same once you understand and acknowledge your own reservoir of strength. Take a moment to "time travel" into your past. Go back through your life and pick out the three most difficult experiences you have faced, such as being unjustly accused of something, losing something or someone precious to you, or facing a particularly embarrassing situation. Write down any crisis situations you have experienced in your past, no matter how great or small.

Difficult Experience 1

_____

_____

Difficult Experience 2

_____

_____

Difficult Experience 3

_____

_____

Now that you have thought of three difficult experiences, relax for a few moments and visualize yourself moving through the experience, step by step. Remember how you felt and what you did. Jot down your feelings and behavior during those crises.

Feelings and behavior during Difficult Experience 1

_____

_____

_____

_____

_____

Feelings and behavior during Difficult Experience 2

_____

_____

_____

_____

_____

Feelings and behavior during Difficult Experience 3

_____

_____

_____

_____

_____

   Those experiences did not destroy you. As you look
back at the past from the point of view of the present,
you have greater perspective to judge the impact of
those situations. You are still alive and probably emo-

tionally stronger because of what you learned during those crises. As time passed, you probably acted with a higher sense of purpose and were able to muster greater strength to overcome the difficulties. Not only did you overcome them, but you may have gained personal confidence in your toughness to meet even the most difficult problems.

People grow from their experiences. Almost all natural-disaster victims believe their experience made them better people. Furthermore, most victims felt surprised at the amount of strength they were able to summon up to face the situation. Those who were not surprised had had earlier experiences that allowed them to believe in their own personal power before they were tested by disaster. This shows that people have the strength when they need it.

Planning for personal growth does not mean that you have to wait for a crisis. Rather, it involves assessing your personal fortitude, strengthening it, and being prepared to profit from whatever happens. The following questions will help you assess your current level of emotional toughness and your prospects for benefiting from unpleasant situations. Take a moment to answer them.

1. In the face of personal tragedy, what would you do? Think of something you would consider tragic, then jot down how you would feel and behave. _____

_____

_____

_____

_____

2. Think about receiving upsetting news, then jot down how you would feel and behave. _____

_____

_____

_____

_____

3. When internal pressure builds, how do you feel and behave? _____

_____

_____

_____

_____

BUILDING EMOTIONAL STRENGTH

It helps to think about building personal emotional strength in three steps:

1. *Plan instead of worrying.* Worrying is a cold, illogical process that drains your energy, confuses you, and leads only to unhappiness. It simply does no good. But planning to deal with a

problem or crisis does help you use your energy constructively and regard the future as manageable. Planning involves breaking down the problem and sorting through its various aspects, setting and organizing goals, and, finally, doing your best to cope. Planning works better than worrying because it is a constructive rather than destructive use of energy.

2. *Dispute your powerless beliefs.* Feelings of powerlessness result from telling yourself such things as, "I'm weak and incompetent" or "I just don't know if I will be able to handle this situation." You can dispute powerless beliefs by changing that kind of self-talk to powerful self-talk such as, "I know that I have a reservoir of strength that I can call upon when I need to."

3. *Rehearse success.* Visualize yourself successfully solving problems by planning and acting rationally. Two benefits result from such visualization: you get the practice of working through the problem, and you build a feeling of confidence.

SUCCESS JOURNAL

The following exercises are organized to help you realize more fully that you are an emotionally strong person. Use them as a journal over the next seven days or do them as an exercise in one sitting.

To Do Today	Rank	Commitments

Success Journal

Think for a few minutes about how much time you spend worrying. Convince yourself that worrying does not help; tell yourself that you will worry less and plan more in the future.

To Do Today	Rank	Commitments

Success Journal

Spend a few minutes thinking about a time when you faced a problem with courage and toughness. Give yourself credit for being a courageous and strong person.

To Do Today	Rank	Commitments

Success Journal

"Operant conditioning" is a principle of learning that says people learn to do things better when they are reinforced for doing them. Have you rewarded yourself for the good and noble things you have done?

To Do Today	Rank	Commitments

Success Journal

Acknowledge the strength you used today in handling some difficult situation. Use this to increase powerful self-talk.

To Do Today	Rank	Commitments

Success Journal

"Time travel" into some future moment. Imagine receiving bad news. Now imagine handling the situation successfully.

To Do Today	Rank	Commitments

Success Journal

Take a problem you are facing and break it into many small problems. Now write down what you will do—what action you will take relative to each small aspect of the larger problem.

To Do Today	Rank	Commitments

Success Journal

Note how you feel now that you have begun planning instead of worrying. Do you have more energy? Do you feel more productive? Are you achieving more?

RECOMMENDED READING

McMullin, R. E., and Casy, W. W. *Talk Sense to Yourself*. Denver: Jefferson Mental Health Center, 1977. This basic outline for cognitive restructuring attempts to help the reader quickly identify and overcome irrational thoughts with positive self-knowledge. The book is simple and very readable.

Rubin, T. I. *Compassion and Self-Hate: An Alternative to Despair*. New York: McKay, 1975. In this book Rubin analyzes the dominant cause of much human suffering: self-hate. He presents a highly effective therapy for it. This book is highly analytical but thoroughly readable and is a basic text in self-help.

tomorrow is not good enough

"Taking time to deal with problems enhances my psychological strength and affords me more time to grow" is the fourth growth-producing belief.

The motto of the procrastinator is: Never do today what you can put off until tomorrow. At first that sounds good, but procrastination leads to a buildup of unfinished business. It is not a good way to get along with ourselves or other people.

People often procrastinate when they have to do things that cause anxiety or discomfort, such as returning a defective item to a store, doing difficult household chores, facing an angry person, or risking criticism from a loved one. These things may make you feel inadequate or vulnerable. But if you respond by trying to avoid the task, you are only procrastinating.

Procrastination produces that bugaboo—unfinished business. Unfinished business leads to a nagging feeling that robs you of joy and vitality and makes you feel guilty and incompetent. It is like carrying around excess baggage: it makes you tired and prevents your reaching your destination. As your list of unfinished business grows, you begin to dislike yourself and may eventually come to feel unworthy or unable to cope with life. In extreme cases, unfinished business leads to feelings of depression and worthlessness.

As you prepare your "To Do Today" list, make sure you include your unfinished business. Do not push it to the back of your mind and let it sit there, ripping off your good feelings. Unfinished business is to be treated the same way as other items on the "To Do Today" list. You will be amazed at how well you feel when you move your unfinished business from your "To Do Today" list to your Success Journal.

DETERMINING UNFINISHED BUSINESS

Take a couple of minutes right now to think of three tasks about which you are procrastinating and which are now unfinished business. These might be easy tasks, such as taking out the trash; or they might be harder tasks, such as being more assertive about your rights. List the three tasks in the space below.

Task 1

_____

_____

Task 2

_____

_____

Task 3

_____

_____

Most of us give ourselves reasons for putting off a task. "Oh, I can do that tomorrow. I'll have more time then." Freud called this process "rationalization." Whether we call it an excuse, a reason, or a rationalization, we are in reality trying to avoid feeling guilty.

Reasons for procrastination may reflect different levels of understanding. If you say "I can do it tomorrow when I have more time," that is one thing; but if you say "I won't do it today because I don't know how," that is something else indeed. One reason often masks another. "I can do it tomorrow" might be what you _think_ you mean; but "I'm afraid that I won't be able to do it" suggests a whole different problem and solution. If you examine why you choose to procrastinate, you may discover that you will continue to do so until you acquire some new skills.

Most procrastination includes some strong emotion as a motivating force. Other emotions enter after you have procrastinated. You might procrastinate to avoid some feeling of discomfort or fear, but later you begin to feel guilty and unworthy. These feelings complicate the process of procrastination and give unfinished business a sting. For example, you may put off doing housework or writing letters because you "don't feel like it," but once you have dismissed the task, another feeling creeps in giving rise to "I'm guilty" or "I'm lazy."

It is important to sort out the reasons you procrastinate and how you feel about it. For practice, take a few minutes to look at the tasks you named above and try to sort them out for yourself.

Task 1

What reasons do you give yourself for not doing this task? _____

_____

_____

What are your feelings about this task? _____

_____

_____

Task 2

Write down what you say to give yourself permission for putting off this task. _____

_____

_____

_____

As you wrote the above, did it stir up feelings of anger, guilt, fear, or anxiety? Write down the feelings associated with not doing this task. _____

_____

_____

_____

Task 3

What do you tell yourself about this task?_____

_____

_____

_____

What feelings are linked with your procrastination as
regards this task? _____

_____

_____

What patterns did you detect in your reasons or in your
feelings as you examined your three cases? _____

_____

_____

_____

_____

_____

CLEARING THE AIR

There are two ways to finish off unfinished business. First, you can assess the importance of the task. If
it involves your welfare or the welfare of others , make
specific plans for finishing it. More about this later in
the chapter.

A second approach is to examine the task at hand and conclude that if you never finished it, no one would be hurt. If that is the case, by all means give yourself permission to forget it. Do not spend another moment thinking or worrying about it. While this should not be construed as permission to casually wipe out all unfinished business, it is a recognition that your goals and dreams change and, consequently, what is important changes also. If you try to dismiss an item of unfinished business but have nagging doubts about doing so, reexamine it; you may have missed something.

At this point, take a few moments to analyze the three tasks you listed as unfinished business. What is likely to happen if you give yourself permission to forget one or more of them? Will that seriously affect you or anyone else? Would you *be able* to simply dismiss the task when it is reasonable to do so? Now list the likely consequences of doing or not doing any of the three unfinished tasks.

Task 1

_____

_____

_____

Task 2

_____

_____

_____

Task 3

_____

_____

_____

FINISHING UNFINISHED BUSINESS

You have gone through the process of making plans toward reaching your important life goals; you can use this same process to make plans toward ridding yourself of unfinished business. Think through your tasks. Make specific plans for finishing them by noting how and when you are going to attack each one.

Task 1

_____

_____

_____

Task 2

_____

_____

_____

Task 3

_____

_____

_____

Sydney Harris has said: "A winner takes a big problem and separates it into smaller parts so that it can be more easily manipulated; a loser takes a lot of little problems and rolls them together until they are unsolvable." Take a few minutes and list as many items of unfinished business as you can. List them, not as a loser does (little problems rolled together into an unsolvable problem) but as a winner does (big problem separated into smaller parts that can be solved or dismissed). _____

_____

_____

_____

ACQUIRING NECESSARY SKILLS

Procrastination is often linked with the level of skill required to deal competently with a task and the possession of the necessary tools to complete it. We might *think* we can fix a leaky faucet, but we are unsure how to begin. It may be necessary to learn a new skill even though it will prove time-consuming and often discouraging.

Dealing with procrastination includes planning ways to acquire tools and skills needed to complete a task. Sometimes we need to acquire physical as well as mental tools.

Check through each task you listed previously and analyze it for the feelings and reasons that surround it. Decide which tasks can be dismissed; dismiss those. The remaining tasks require some action, so make some specific plans to deal with them. First, decide what tools and skills are needed and whether or not you have them. Next, set a target date for the completion of your unfinished business. Take enough time to think carefully about any tasks that will be especially difficult to attack.

Unfinished Business 1 _____

_____

Tools needed _____

_____

Skills needed _____

_____

Target date for completion _____

Unfinished Business 2 _____

_____

Tools needed _____

_____

Skills needed _____

_____

Target date for completion _____

Unfinished Business 3 _____

_____

Tools needed _____

_____

Skills needed _____

_____

Target date for completion _____

Unfinished Business 4 _____

_____

Tools needed _____

_____

Skills needed _____

_____

Target date for completion _____

Unfinished Business 5 _____

_____

Tools needed _____

_____

Skills needed _____

_____

Target date for completion _____

Unfinished Business 6 _____

_____

Tools needed _____

_____

Skills needed _____

_____

Target date for completion _____

Unfinished Business 7 _____

_____

Tools needed _____

_____

Skills needed _____

_____

Target date for completion _____

SUCCESS JOURNAL

Be sure that these items of unfinished business are entered on your "To Do Today" list on the appropriate days. Once they are completed, they should be listed as successes in your daily Success Journal. Complete the following exercises in the next seven days.

To Do Today	Rank	Commitments

Success Journal

Some problems are easily solved when we have the proper skills and tools. Think of the skills and tools you might need to solve a problem in your life and make plans to acquire them.

To Do Today	Rank	Commitments

Success Journal

Do you reward yourself when you exercise the self-discipline needed to solve problems? What rewards might you give yourself for working on problems?

To Do Today	Rank	Commitments

Success Journal

What do you tell yourself about problems you would like to avoid? For the next week, repeat growth-producing belief number 4: "Taking time to deal with problems enhances my psychological strength and affords me more time to grow." You may want to rewrite this belief in your own words.

To Do Today	Rank	Commitments

Success Journal

Identify some problem that you face on a regular basis and make plans to solve it.

To Do Today	Rank	Commitments

Success Journal

Reflect upon the good feelings you experienced upon completion of some important task. Note, also, the strength you gained.

To Do Today	Rank	Commitments

Success Journal

Many problems are more easily solved when we work on them with other people. Pick a task and list the people who would benefit themselves and you by the mutual effort.

To Do Today	Rank	Commitments

Success Journal

Sometimes problems seem bigger than they really are. We can cut them down to size by analyzing them step by step. Analyze the steps necessary in solving one of your problems and note how it becomes more manageable.

RECOMMENDED READING

Harris, S. *Winners & Losers*. Niles, Ill.: Argus, 1973. Winners and losers are here contrasted through illustrations and cogent captions. The book is fun to read and provides insights into how best to cope with daily hassles.

Lembo, J. *Help Yourself*. Niles, Ill.: Argus, 1974. A well-written book about the meaning of personal relationships, our relationship with our environment, the development of personal goals, and the importance of our personal thoughts. Thoughts can be translated into greater self-acceptance and mistakes can lead to learning.

time travel

Time is one of the most interesting and exciting concepts to contemplate. It is not easy to comprehend, but it is a very important part of each of us. We cannot control time, but we can control some of the influence it has over us by controlling the ways we think about it and the ways we think about ourselves *in* time.

Sometimes we live in the past because it is a secure, familiar place to be, filled with accomplishments and good connections with other people. Other times we live in the past because we cannot get away from all the errors we have made that cause us to feel unhappy and guilty—all the things we "should have done" or "should not have done." When we live with those "shoulds," the past dominates the present in a cruel way, limiting us and cutting us off from productive and creative ways of life.

Sometimes we fear things in the future. When we do, we let something that does not exist interfere with our lives. Often we grant that feared event a reality, a magnitude that it will never have on its own. We may fear failure in our friendships, in school, or in our jobs—or at least fear that we will not be as successful as we would like to be. It is like a tragicomedy. What is more absurd than being afraid of something that does not

exist? What can be more tragic than a life of possible joy lost through fear and anxiety?

The growth-producing belief you will explore in this chapter is: "I am at my best when I live in the present and plan for, rather than dread, the future; when I derive strength and pleasure, rather than guilt, from the past." Your past is gone, but it can offer guidance in the present when you capitalize upon what you have learned, gain insight from mistakes, and find out how to dismiss those haunting ghosts from yesteryear. The future can help you live a better today when you regard it as a "light at the end of a tunnel" rather than as some scary, dark, and unknown place filled with danger.

DEALING WITH THE PAST AND THE FUTURE

Ask yourself the following questions: "Have I been unable to deal with feelings of guilt?" "Do I use my childhood as an excuse for feelings of incompetence in the present?" "Do I have fears about bad things that might happen in the future?" "Am I pessimistic about my success in the future?" If you answer "Yes" to these questions, you may be spending too much time in the past or in the future. The following sections will help you learn to enjoy the past and eliminate the debilitating ghosts from both the past and the future.

Dismissing Guilt

In our society guilt is often used to socialize the young. When children act in unconventional ways, parents often shame them and introduce them to the pain of feeling guilty. Your adventure of personal growth may be delayed because of "shoulds" that haunt you from the past and make you feel guilty. The sad thing is that guilt really serves no purpose.

The most senseless guilt comes from some imperfect act you may have performed as a youngster. This guilt is often the most relentless and may infect your total personality.

Some kinds of guilt are simpler. You may lie to avoid an unwanted social engagement, then feel guilty about having done so. Such guilt is natural, but it still must be dealt with since it can affect your feelings about yourself—that you have let somebody down. It can lurk around the edge of your consciousness, stealing the joy from your life or threatening some dire consequence. Guilt is the opposite of a positive, powerful self-concept.

How do you deal with guilt? In theory the answer is simple: just identify it, analyze it, and dismiss it. But in practice it is not quite so simple. Still, with calm and persistent effort you can rid yourself of it.

Identify Your "Shoulds"

Do you often tell yourself that you "should" do this or that or that you "should" be this or that? Use the space below to list one or two things you tell yourself you "should" do or be relative to your physical self, your relationships with others, and your work environment.

The "shoulds" you tell yourself about your physical health and appearance:

_____

_____

_____

_____

The "shoulds" you tell yourself about your relationships with your family and friends:

_____

_____

_____

_____

The "shoulds" you tell yourself about your work or schooling:

_____

_____

_____

_____

Like most of us, you carry a couple of complex images of yourself. One is an image of who you **are**. The other is an image of who you **should** be. The discrepancy between those two images is what causes feelings of guilt. The very fact that guilt results from this discrepancy gives you a key to dealing with it. One approach is to examine your perceptions of who you "should" be, clarify them, and challenge each of them by asking yourself who you really choose to be according to the self-analysis you have already done in earlier chapters. In the following spaces, rewrite the statements you tell yourself about who you should be by replacing the word "should" with the phrases "I choose to" or "I choose not to." For instance, if under "your physical health" you wrote, "I should get more exercise," change that statement to "I choose to get more exercise."

Choices you make about your physical health and appearance:

_____

_____

_____

_____

_____

Choices you make about your relationships with your family and friends:

_____

_____

_____

_____

_____

Choices you make about your work or schooling:

_____

_____

_____

_____

_____

To continue this analysis, ask yourself this question: "Do I have a commitment to changing my behavior in some significant way?" Think through each choice you stated above. If you have no commitment to change, tell yourself: "I have no commitment to change at this time; therefore I'm not going to feel guilty about it." If you do feel a commitment, say to yourself: "Yes, I do have a commitment to change my behavior." In either case, guilt will not help. What will help is acknowledging your undesirable behavior and making plans to change it.

THE DESIRE FOR PUNISHMENT

Many people live with the belief that guilt deserves punishment. If you feel that you have done some things that deserve punishment, write the "crime" and appropriate punishment on the lines below.

Crime: _____

Punishment: _____

154

Crime: _____

Punishment: _____

Crime: _____

Punishment: _____

As you look at the deserved punishment, ask yourself the following questions: "If I receive that punishment, who will benefit from it?" "Will I be a better person after being punished?"

For the most part, continued punishment for past wrongdoings saps the joy of today and becomes a stumbling block instead of a stepping-stone to your personal growth. If you feel the need for some punishment for previous wrongdoings, take some time to write down something positive you can do that will benefit other people and yourself—something that can be considered a "constructive option." For example, you may want to make a contribution to some charitable cause, volunteer your time to a worthy organization, or make an apology to someone that would help them and you in the long run.

Write your constructive options here:

1. _____

_____

2. _____

   _____

3. _____

   _____

The need to punish yourself is based upon the irrational belief that if you suffer enough, you will atone for some wrongdoing or mistake. Such a notion should be replaced with the belief that most of your bad, destructive, antisocial behavior comes from an immature part of you that fails to understand the consequences of an act or the nature of a positive, loving relationship with other human beings.

BUILDING A POSITIVE FUTURE

As a human being, you have the ability to travel through time in your fantasies. You can travel into the past by imagining or remembering events of long ago, both frightening and pleasurable. There is an added degree of freedom when you move into the future since it has not yet taken place and you can still influence it. In a sense, you can create different futures by building different scenarios (brief outlines of events). Some of these scenarios might describe you as competent and successful, while others might picture you as a failure. Success scenarios generate feelings of optimism and power, while failure scenarios breed pessimism and fear.

The following exercise can help you build positive scenarios of the future:

1. Select some growth project that you have found particularly hard to start. It may be something like losing weight, meeting new friends, or learning some new skill. Write it here:

   _____

I WILL BE A THIN SUCCESSFUL FANTASTIC HUMAN BEING

---

2. Build a scenario for yourself by first listing all the benefits you might experience from the project, then listing all the inconveniences or sufferings you might experience. The following is an example of such a listing by a person who wanted to start a diet.

Benefits	Inconveniences
Lose weight Be more attractive Live longer Feel better, more vital Forestall disease Wear fashionable clothing	1. Feel deprived and hungry 2. Be embarrassed at parties 3. Might promise self things and not deliver them, for example, weight loss 4. Might get sick

Make a similar list of benefits and inconveniences you might experience from your own growth project.

Benefits	Inconveniences

Now, in your imagination, project yourself into the future and imagine yourself being successful and enjoying all the benefits gained from your growth project. Imagine yourself the way you would like to be. Explore the fantasy and make it as vivid as you can.

Practice visiting the future in this positive way. It can be an especially useful tool when you dread some upcoming event. Project yourself into the future and see yourself enjoying the benefits rather than struggling with the inconveniences you might experience.

LIVING IN THE PRESENT

Living in the now—building an awareness and sensitivity to the now—is like living in a house with many rooms. It is a place to which you can retreat and find rest and safety from the things that plague you. It is a place where you can rebuild yourself. It is a place of new beginnings. It is a home.

The present is a good place to be for many reasons. It is a place where you can abandon your anxieties and reestablish your internal balance. It is a place where you can find yourself and discover who you are and how you are connected to others. You can look at the future from the present and choose your destination consciously and wisely, without fear or trepidation.

SUCCESS JOURNAL

Use the following pages to explore your understanding of time and "time travel."

To Do Today	Rank	Commitments

Success Journal

Growth-producing belief number 5 is: "I am at my best when I live in the present and plan for, rather than dread, the future; when I derive strength and pleasure, rather than guilt, from the past." Rewrite this belief in your own words and repeat it to yourself during the week.

To Do Today	Rank	Commitments

Success Journal

When you feel tense, relax as fully as you can and focus upon your physical sensations. Do not think about threats and fears from the past or in the future. Does this help you cope with problems? Note what kinds of relaxation work best for you.

To Do Today	Rank	Commitments

Success Journal

You can bring the future into the present through "time travel." Relax and imagine yourself at your best in some future situation. What events and decisions promise to give you a happy and stimulating future?

To Do Today	Rank	Commitments

Success Journal

Ask yourself what is bothering you most right now. First, imagine the worst thing that could happen; next, imagine the best that could happen to you in that situation. What can you do to enhance the likelihood of the best thing happening?

To Do Today	Rank	Commitments

Success Journal

Think of the most exciting and pleasant event in your past. Recreate it in the present as vividly as you can. Note the feelings you experienced and the optimism, connectedness, or power you gained.

To Do Today	Rank	Commitments

Success Journal

You are a one-time happening in all the universe, and because of that you are irreplaceable and precious. Set aside the fears and worries of the past and the future and note some of the powers you have just because you are a human being.

To Do Today	Rank	Commitments

Success Journal

Note all of the things you accomplished today that would have gone undone if you had not existed.

RECOMMENDED READING

Benson, H. *The Relaxation Response*. New York: Avon, 1976. The author describes how to relax and lists the healthful benefits that accompany learning how to rid ourselves of tension and stress. Both readable and concise, the book provides nontechnical presentations of several approaches to relaxation.

Keyes, K., Jr. *Handbook to Higher Consciousness*. Berkeley, Calif.: Living Love Center, 1975. This book analyzes levels of consciousness and points out pathways to freeing the mind. It is a practical manual for people who are interested in becoming more aware of the "here and now." Easy reading about a sometimes difficult subject.

cherishing your environment

The literature of psychology often looks at the individual as apart from the environment. However, we all know that we are dependent upon our environment in several important ways. Our physical existence, for instance, is dependent upon warmth, food, and oxygen. When we lack any one of these elements, we die. The sixth growth-producing belief is about the environment: "My growth is best promoted by recognizing my connectedness with my environment."

BEING CONNECTED TO YOUR ENVIRONMENT

You are psychologically connected to both your social and physical environments. If you are accepted, admired, and supported in your social environment, you feel confident and secure. If you live in a supportive physical environment, you feel healthy and energetic. On the other hand, if you are attacked and rejected in your social environment or live in an ugly physical environment, you must spend much of your energy just coping with or defending yourself against potential dangers.

Consider your environments for a few moments. Are they supportive or are they enfeebling? Jot down ways your environments help or hinder.

1. My social environment helps me in these ways.

_____

_____

_____

2. My social environment hinders me in these ways.

_____

_____

_____

3. My physical environment helps me in these ways.

_____

_____

_____

4. My physical environment hinders me in these ways. _____

_____

_____

169

You are connected to your environment in another important way. You cause things to happen in it. Your actions can affect your social environment by causing people to treat you in either supportive or nonsupportive ways. How you manage your physical environment can be either supportive or nonsupportive of your growth. If you choose to live with disorder and chaos, you may find yourself thinking and acting in disordered ways. Living with ugliness may cause you to feel ugly. You are part of your physical environment, which means that you can develop a love or a hate relationship with it. Your surroundings reflect something about you and how you feel about yourself. Treating your environment with care and concern is a way of expressing your care and concern for yourself. Abusing your environment is a form of self-abuse which will take away your pride and the support of others.

Ask yourself the following questions and jot down your answers in a few words.

1. What do my clothes say about me? _____

_____

_____

2. How do my living quarters reflect my feelings about myself?
   (Are they usually clean or messy? Colorful or drab? Inviting or intimidating to others?)

_____

_____

_____

3. What do I say or do that make others support or reject me? _____

_____

There is yet another, more elusive relationship you have with your environment. You find meaning and fulfillment in your life according to what you expect from your environment. If you expect that only a "perfect" environment will fulfill your life, you are bound to be disappointed. Some people may think of fulfillment as living in a little white house with a white picket fence and a car in the garage; others might see fulfillment in a splendid penthouse apartment. But fulfillment and contentment come only when you have a sense of confidence in dealing with reality and when you establish a loving and creative relationship with your environment. You create fulfillment with yourself. A positive environment merely supports it and adds to it. Intentional personal growth involves developing your human potential and creating the best physical surroundings you can. Fully functioning individuals love themselves and their surroundings. They demonstrate it by making the most of themselves and their environment.

SUCCESS JOURNAL

Use the following Success Journal for the next seven days.

To Do Today	Rank	Commitments

Success Journal

Your very existence means that your environment is sustaining. What have you done today that positively promotes your environment?

To Do Today	Rank	Commitments

Success Journal

Growth-producing belief number 6 is: "My growth is best promoted by recognizing my connectedness with my environment." Rewrite this belief in your own words and repeat it to yourself during the week.

To Do Today	Rank	Commitments

Success Journal

Think of one thing you can do today to improve or beautify your physical environment.

To Do Today	Rank	Commitments

Success Journal

Your social environment is extremely important. Note one thing you did today that promoted a more positive social environment.

To Do Today	Rank	Commitments

Success Journal

Note how you have shown care, love, or appreciation for your environment.

To Do Today	Rank	Commitments

Success Journal

You enhance yourself when you look at and appreciate the beauty around you. Take some time to notice something beautiful in your environment. Make a note of it.

To Do Today	Rank	Commitments

Success Journal

Relax and imagine an environment that would nourish and support your intentional personal growth. What have you done today to help create such an environment?

commitment to life-long growth

The seventh and final growth-producing belief is a kind of summary of the others; for that reason, it is an important one: "I maximize my growth by learning, doing, and creating as well as by profiting from my mistakes, cherishing my successes, and having a willingness to make growth decisions."

The human organism seeks to reduce or avoid tension and anxiety. This drive sometimes leads to a belief detrimental to personal growth: "I can avoid all anxiety and tension by avoiding all hassles and by not taking any risks." The short-term benefits of this belief are overshadowed by the long-term consequences of living a passive, powerless, and dull life. Such a belief destroys strength of character, self-respect, and the ability to grow. It separates you from your environment and the people around you, causing you to perceive your surroundings as powerful and yourself as weak.

LEARNING IS MAGIC

One of the most magical things in life is learning. The infant who cannot yet talk will become a poet; the child who cannot yet walk will become an Olympic athlete— all through the magic of learning.

You develop your potential and become a fully functioning human being insofar as you commit yourself to

life-long learning. Think of all the skills you have developed since you were an infant. Why, then, should you stop learning now? Learning makes it easier to deal with the world. It helps you choose destinations and goals and shows you how to achieve them. Learning can also help you develop your potential for creativity.

Write down three things you have learned about yourself as a result of doing the exercises in this book:

1. _____

2. _____

3. _____

Now write down three growth-producing skills you have mastered or almost mastered within the past two weeks:

1. _____

2. _____

3. _____

Name other items of self-knowledge or other skills you *want* to master during the remainder of this year:

_____

_____

_____

_____

_____

CREATING AND GROWING

Creativity is expressed by having the courage to think about, do, and make things in new ways. It is a positive engagement of the powers of thought and visualization. As one of the highest powers of the human intellect, it is also one of the most pleasing and satisfying human characteristics. Creativity produces growth because it channels spontaneity and energy into new projects. It is what sets the growing person apart.

Creativity often results in mistakes, however. If you try to do something new, you run the risk of failing or having to try again and again. You can let mistakes overwhelm you, or you can learn from them and use them as powerful teachers. Some people overlook their own mistakes or try to blame them on others. They avoid situations, people, and places where they have made mistakes in the past; as a consequence, their world continually becomes smaller and more restricted rather than expansive and flexible. If, however, you choose to learn from your mistakes, you grow in a

special way; you turn your weaknesses into strengths and constantly increase your capacities, skills, and knowledge.

You have the daily opportunity to choose between playing it safe by taking no risks or making creative growth decisions with the possibility of failure or error. A "safe" decision means you opt to live life as carefully and cautiously as you can. The result is stifling. You will wind up doing routine things in routine ways, making your days boring and monotonous.

On the other hand, creative growth decisions lead you into new and exciting paths, stretch your potential, and strengthen your assertiveness to strive for a better and more challenging life. They can generate stimulating, interesting, and productive days in which you will learn new skills, expand your personal boundaries, and have more to offer yourself and society. Growth decisions take courage, but the rewards are well worth it.

Fill in the following chart as a review of decisions you have recently made, mistakes that have resulted, and experiences you have gained from those mistakes.

Growth Decisions
Mistakes
Learning Experiences

A good deal of space in each chapter has been devoted to the process of cherishing your successes. Because you attend to only a part of your experience, you often do not credit yourself for the good and noble things you accomplish. Consequently your overall picture of yourself is that of a limited person. Learning to cherish successes is a basic growth skill that is first practiced by keeping a Success Journal, then using it to change your self-talk.

SUCCESS JOURNAL

The Success Journal has been presented in different forms throughout this book. It is to be hoped that you have learned to use it to contribute to your growth. Your task is to create your own journal—one that is tailored to your own purposes and your own particular growth needs. Keep a journal of the experiences that are important to you; record ideas, events, and experiences from your reading, your travel, and your encounters with others. Create your own growth projects based upon your self-confidence and your own insights. In that way, you will continue to grow at an increasing rate.

To Do Today	Rank	Commitments

Success Journal

We expand our boundaries and further our growth by challenging our fears and limitations. What have you done today that enhanced your psychological strength?

To Do Today	Rank	Commitments

Success Journal

Every decision we make either stretches us and helps us grow or promotes the status quo by reinforcing our safety. What growth decisions have you made in the last twenty-four hours?

To Do Today	Rank	Commitments

Success Journal

Rewrite the following belief in your own words:
"I maximize my growth by learning, doing, and creating as
well as by profiting from my mistakes, cherishing my
successes, and having a willingness to make growth
decisions." Repeat your restatement of the belief daily
during the next week.

To Do Today	Rank	Commitments

Success Journal

A winner learns from his or her mistakes, while a loser overlooks or hides them. Note the mistakes you have made today and jot down what you have learned from them.

To Do Today	Rank	Commitments

Success Journal

Cherishing successes builds self-confidence and gives us a realistic image of ourselves. It is, therefore, crucial to our personal growth. Note all your successes in the last twenty-four hours.

Date Today _____

To Do Today	Rank	Commitments

Success Journal

List all the new things you learned today. Sort through all your experiences so that you do not miss anything. Note how they enrich your life.

189

To Do Today	Rank	Commitments

Success Journal

Your life is precious, and you are in charge of it. In the long run you can be who you choose to be. What are your long-term growth plans, and what are you doing to promote them?

Remember, your growth is dependent upon your envisioning it in vivid and realistic ways, planning for it, and persistently pursuing it.